# JEWISH COINS

# JEWISH COINS

BY

THÉODORE REINACH

TRANSLATED BY
MARY HILL

WITH AN APPENDIX BY
G. F. HILL

ARGONAUT, INC., PUBLISHERS

CHICAGO　　　　　MCMLXVI

# PREFACE TO THE FIRST AMERICAN EDITION

The continuously increasing interest in recent years in ancient as well as modern Jewish numismatics makes it necessary now, more than at any time in the past, to make available the standard works on the subject. Theodore Reinach's *Jewish Coins*, by virtue of the fact that such a renown numismatist as George F. Hill deemed it worthy of translation from the French original and that it has remained the best introduction to Jewish coinage for over half a century, is now reissued for the use of students and collectors of the coins of ancient and modern Israel.

It is a fact that sixty three years have passed since the first edition of *Jewish Coins* and the study of Jewish numismatics has advanced at an admirable pace, but except for the valuable handbook *Ancient Jewish Coins* by the late professor A. Reifenberg, the excellent *Corpus Nummorum Palaestinensiam* (four volumes published to date) and a substantial number of articles and monographs examining many important subjects and problems in the field, there is no other English language book on Jewish coins readily available to the public. Now, with the great interest in the coins of the new state of Israel, as well as the earlier ancient Palestinian numismatic tradition, there

# PREFACE

is an obvious need for reference material on the subject. In Israel today, the scholars, as well as the youth, are taking an unprecedented interest in both archaeology and numismatics to the point that these studies might be considered the national pastime. This enthusiasm for the study of coins has inevitably spread abroad and will undoubtedly continue to so in even greater measure.

Reinach's *Jewish Coins* was the first book which exposed me to the field of numismatics as an excellent aid to the study of history and I believe that many others beside myself have profited from this book since 1903. The brilliant introduction, one of the most vigorous texts ever written, I believe, explaining the value of the study of numismatics, has remained permanently engraved in my memory. If only for the sake of this part of the work, this book will be valuable for the younger generations and the historians of tomorrow.

Thanks to the dedicated work of the late Professor Adolf Reifenberg, new horizons are opened today to the students of ancient Jewish history and numismatics. The types and issues of the Hasmonean dynasty (167-37 BCE) are now better known than in the time of Reinach and the same can be said for those of the Herodian dynasty (37 BCE-94 CE) and the Jewish -Roman War (66-73 CE). Reifenberg's greatest contribution, in my judgment, is that from the study of the hoard of silver coins from Siwan, he finally established the date of issue for the Hebrew shekels at the period of revolt of Bar Kochba (66-73 CE) instead of the period of Simon the Hasmonean (142-

# PREFACE

135 BCE) to which they had been assigned by earlier scholars.

Reifenberg's *Ancient Jewish Coins* is without doubt the best modern handbook of Jewish numismatics and its use by the student and scholar as the first reference is essential. However, in some details, and especially in literary style and enthusiasm, it has not superseded Reinach's text, and in some cases, the conservative views of the latter are more acceptable to the historian. For example, in the case of the beginnings of Jewish coinage, even today the majority agrees with Reinach who definitely excludes the periods before the Maccabaeans. Reifenberg tried to prove that the beginnings could be traced to the age of Persian Rule (538-332 BCE) and proposed the identification of a crude silver imitation of the Athenian tetradrachm as the earliest Jewish coin struck by Nehemia. But the possibility that the Jews at such an early date might have accepted coins with representations opposed to their law is remote in my humble opinion.

With the help of the present reissue of Reinach's *Jewish Coins,* I hope that the new generation of students of Jewish numismatics will be able to arrive at new levels of achievement by combining the best of the most recent scholarship and the conservatism of the earlier work of Reinach.

DR. ABRAHAM SILVERSTEIN

LOS ANGELES
MAY 1966

# PREFACE

I⊤ is unnecessary to apologize for the introduction to the English-reading public of M. Théodore Reinach's little work on Jewish coins. Our thanks are due to him, as well as to his publisher, M. Leroux, for permission to publish the translation, which has been made by my wife, and revised by the author both in manuscript and proof. In many respects it differs from the original edition, especially in regard to the *crux* of Jewish Numismatics, the question of the *shekels*. The passages relating to this matter have been entirely rewritten by the author, who has found reason to change his

## PREFACE

views. I have also to thank him, as well as Messrs. Bemrose and Sons, for permission to add as an Appendix the greater part of an article, previously published in the *Reliquary and Illustrated Archæologist*, on the current forgery of the Jewish shekel.

G. F. HILL.

*British Museum,*
*June 1903.*

# LIST OF PLATES

## ERRATA.

Page 7, note 2 : *for* ἀφείλετε *read* ὀφείλετε.

Page 16, note 1, *ad fin.* : *for* " abolished " *read* " celebrated."

Page 22, note 1 : *read* " Ketuboth."

Page 45, for " *was the independence . . . question* " read " *was the last hope of the independence of Israel destroyed.*"

# INTRODUCTION

ALTHOUGH the science of Numismatics was one of the earliest branches of archaeology to attract students, it has never yet succeeded in gaining the favour of the general public. Their opportunities of seeing interesting coins are rare, and when they hear anything about them it is generally due to the exorbitant prices fetched by them at sales. They are therefore only. too readily disposed to regard numismatists as people afflicted with the collector's mania, and their pretended science as a mere hobby to be placed in the same category with the collecting of autographs, postcards, or military buttons.

I do not propose to undertake here the defence of *numismatists ;* they are, moreover, far too deeply absorbed in the jealous contemplation of their treasures to trouble themselves about the good or evil which is spoken of them. But I should like to protest against the unjust contempt of which *Numismatics* is the object, and to begin by showing in a few words that it is a true science, and one of the most precious aids to historical research.

Let us suppose, to take a concrete example, that 2000 years hence, when the civilization of which we are so proud is extinct and almost forgotten, some scholar happens to find a specimen of a sovereign of King Edward VII. Can we not imagine that with a little perspicacity he might draw from it the most interesting conclusions as to the state of English society at the beginning of the twentieth century?

From an analysis of a bit of the metal he will establish the slightness of the alloy which it contains, and thus recognize the scrupulous honesty of the monetary administration.

An examination of the external appearance of the coin—the flatness of its surfaces, the perfect regularity of its circumference, the uniform thickness of the blank, with its

type and lettering in relief—will lead him to
admire the perfection of our scientific apparatus and our mechanical processes ; while
he will guess that our coins had a large
circulation, and that it must have been
customary to arrange them in piles.

Passing on to an examination of the *types*,
our numismatist will probably be less im-
pressed by the genius of our designers than
by the skill of our workmen. He will
become acquainted with the personal appearance of King Edward VII. As to the
reverse type, it will astonish him that this
coin, bearing the date of the year 1903,
should show a servile reproduction of a type
of the year 1816, when the " horseman" was
first introduced. He will ask himself if it
was really worth while immortalizing the
name of the author of this rather frigid com-
position by letting his signature figure below
his work, a privilege which in antiquity was
granted only to the greatest artists.

Finally, there is the *legend* on the coin. He
will learn from it the form of the British
government in the year 1903, the name of

the reigning sovereign, if by chance all other historical records of the time have disappeared, the extent of the empire (at least if he properly resolves the abbreviations BRITT. OMN. and IND. IMP.), the monotheistic principle of the national religion (D(EI) G(RATIA)), the ecclesiastical character assigned by the constitution to the head of the State (F. D.), and last, not least, the persistent influence of the classical, especially the Roman, culture on the higher English education as well as the conservative spirit, owing to which the monetary legends were drawn up in an obsolete language, unknown to ninety-nine out of a hundred people expected to handle the coin.

To sum up, economic, industrial, and scientific conditions, the prosperity of the arts, government, religion, national education, there is not one side of our civilization upon which this small piece of gold, for us only a commonplace medium of exchange, may not one day serve to throw light. Now what the coins of to-day will be for the scholars of the year 4000, that the coins of

2000 years ago are for our scholars of to-day
—an inexhaustible source of authentic information of all kinds for the vast inquiry which
we have instituted concerning the life of the
ancients.

This slight sketch is enough to justify the
deep study of classical numismatics.    But
the coins of which I propose to treat here do
not possess exactly the same kind of interest
as Greek or Roman coins.    The coins of the
Greeks, like all the productions of that
highly-gifted people, are especially valuable
for their beauty ; they present, in miniature,
a complete history of Greek art.    As to
Roman coins, we have in them, above all, an
incomparable gallery of historical portraits.
In Jewish numismatics we must look neither
for masterpieces nor for portraits.    The
engravers of Jewish coins were very in-
different artists, and the principal resource
of their art, the reproduction of the human
figure or of animal form, was denied them by
the strict observance of the command in the
Decalogue, " Thou shalt not make to thyself
any graven image, nor the likeness of any-

thing that is in the heaven above, or in the earth beneath, or in the waters under the earth." But to compensate for this, Jewish coins offer, from the very severity of their types, a faithful picture of the profoundly religious but indifferently artistic people who created them. The characters in which the legends are written are of the greatest interest as regards the history of the alphabet. Even the variations in the inscriptions and types, however restricted the circle in which they move, reflect the different influences under which Judaism has passed, with its alternations of independence and servitude, of enthusiasm and apathy. Finally, there are many coins, both among Jewish coins properly so called, and among the Greek or Roman coins which relate to events of Jewish history, which throw light upon and complete or correct the information possessed by historians. If we add, to quote M. Renan, that Jewish numismatics offers enormous difficulties of classification, and that the attraction of a difficulty to overcome is quite sufficient to interest the scholar apart from the gain of any positive result,[1] we shall admit that this study is perhaps well worth the quarter of an hour's trouble which Pascal refused to philosophy.

[1] Principal works on Jewish numismatics (over and above the general treatises of Eckhel, Mionnet, Lenormant, and Head) : Perez Bayer, *De numis hebraeo-samaritanis* (1781), etc. Cavedoni, *Numismatica biblica* (1849). De Saulcy, *Recherches sur la numismatique judaïque* (1854). Levy, *Geschichte der jüdischen Münzen* (1862). Madden, *History of Jewish Coinage* (1864 ; 2nd edition in 1881 under the title : *Coins of the Jews*). Merzbacher, *Untersuchungen über alte hebräische Münzen* (*Zeitschrift für Numismatik*, Berlin, 1876 foll.). Zuckermann, *Ueber talmudische Münzen und Gewichte*, Berlin, 1862. And numerous articles by these authors and others (Garrucci, De Vogüé, Reichardt, von Sallet, Graetz, Hamburger), scattered about in the different Reviews devoted to numismatics, archaeology, etc. An almost complete bibliography for the years 1849 to 1879 will be found in the second edition of Madden, which may be regarded as a Corpus, though his classification still leaves much to be desired. A good summary of the subject is the article of Mr. A. R. S. Kennedy (Money) in the Edinburgh *Dictionary of the Bible* by Hastings and others (vol. iii., 1900).

# JEWISH COINS

## I

THE history of Jewish coinage does not begin before the Maccabaean period. The reason is obvious. During the greater part of the existence of the old kingdoms of Israel and Judah coined money was unknown; the invention of this medium of exchange is usually and rightly attributed to the Lydian kings, in the course of the seventh century B.C. For a long time the use of it was restricted to the basin of the Archipelago, especially to Lydia and Ionia. Before it had reached the interior of Asia, the kingdom of Judah was destroyed by the Babylonians (587 B.C.); the northern realm had disappeared more than a century before.

B

So there is no room for a national Jewish coinage in the time of the first Temple.

When the Jews were allowed by the Persian kings to return to their old homes and to rebuild the Temple of Jerusalem, the use of coined money was beginning to spread all over Asia; but then another obstacle sprang up to prevent the Jews from striking money of their own. The right of coinage was considered by the ancients as the exclusive privilege of independent communities; it may be said to have been the touchstone of sovereignty. In the vast extent of the empire of the Achaemenidae, very few princes and townships were allowed or usurped such a privilege, nor is there any record of the Jews having ever obtained or even solicited it. Their small community enjoyed practically the use of their own laws and of their own religion under the guidance of a high priest; but they were bound to pay tribute, and were strictly subjected to the authority of the Persian satraps. Moreover, as they were neither a rich nor a trading people, the want of a special coinage did

not arise among them; they were easily
content with using the coins which formed
the common circulation in south-west Asia.
These were the gold *darics* (Pl. I. 1) and
silver *shekels* (sigloi) (Pl. I. 2) used by the
Achaemenidae, and perhaps also the *shekels*
of Phoenician standard issued from the second
half of the fifth century by some large com-
mercial cities of the Syrian coast (Pl. I. 3, 4).
The Macedonian conquest (332 B.C.) did not
alter this state of things. Judaea remained a
tributary community as well under the conqueror himself as under the Macedonian
dynasties which, after his death, ruled suc-
cessively over Southern Syria: the Ptolemies
in the third century B.C., the Seleucidae from
the beginning of the second. The only
change was, that instead of Persian gold and
silver, the medium of exchange now consisted
of the gold staters, silver tetradrachms and
drachms of Alexander, of the Ptolemies, and
of the Seleucidae (Pl. I. 5).

The reader will therefore readily understand why no weight can be laid on any
late Jewish stories which mention coins of

Abraham, Joshua, David or Mardocheus; [1]
these are nothing more than fancy tales,
which even their authors hardly meant to
be taken seriously. As to the numerous
verses in Scripture which mention payments
in shekels, minas or talents in the time
of the Kings, Judges or Patriarchs, so far
as they are not corrupted by more recent
interpolations, they must be understood of
*weighed ingots*, not of coined money: the
name *shekel*—equivalent to the Greek stater
—denoted a *weight unit* (itself the fiftieth
part of the mina, which is the sixtieth of a
talent) before it was used to signify a *coin* of
the same weight. And in all important trans-
actions the balances had been employed for
the weighing of the precious metals used as
a medium of exchange, ever since the system
of single barter had been forsaken as too
inconvenient. In the sacred books written
during the time of the second Temple,
shekels are rarely mentioned; the currency

---

[1] Bereshit Rabba, 39; Talmud Bab. Babakamma,
97, etc.

consists of darics and drachms; these are foreign, not Jewish coins.

The Jews would never perhaps have thought of issuing a national coinage, had it not been for the political changes brought about by the persecutions of Antiochus Epiphanes (Pl. I. 5). This caricature of Joseph II., as he has been well called, in seeking to enforce Hellenism and the Greek religion on all his subjects by methods of violence, instead of letting time and civilization have their own way, provoked a violent reaction of national sentiment in Judaea. A family of heroes, the Maccabees or Hasmonaeans, took the lead of the patriotic and religious movement, and after an eventful strife of thirty years (168–138 B.C.) succeeded not only in ensuring to their brethren the free exercise of their religion, but also in shaking off the political yoke of the Seleucidae and becoming the chiefs of a semi-independent state. This triumph was due partly to the military talents and warlike achievements of the three brothers, Judas (167–161), Jonathan (161–143), and Simon

(143–135); partly to their political skill and early alliance with Rome; last, but not least, to the internal quarrels of the Seleucidae. The successive pretenders to the Syrian crown, always in need of troops and money, purchased the co-operation of the Jewish chieftains by concession after concession, culminating in the final resignation of all but a nominal suzerainty over the Jewish commonwealth.

It is essential to our subject to state briefly, and date as exactly as possible the successive steps which led to the political emancipation of the Jewish state.

The Hasmonaean insurrection began in 168 B.C. After six years' hard fighting, in 162 B.C., the first object of the national party was obtained by the agreement concluded with the regent Lysias, subsequently to the death of Antiochus Epiphanes. By this agreement the Jews were granted the free exercise of their creed, and the fantastic schemes of religious unification were given up by the Syrian government (1 Macc. vi. 60; 2 Macc. i. 25, 31).

In 153 or 152 B.C. King Alexander Balas appointed the head of the national party, Jonathan, to be high priest of the Jews. He also conferred upon him a high title in the court hierarchy, viz. that of "friend of the King" (1 Macc. x. 20). This was changed in 150 B.C. to the still more eminent dignity of "first friend of the King," and Jonathan was named governor and prefect[1] of Judaea (1 Macc. x. 65). In this way the Hasmonaean partisan became practically the master of his native country, but he held the position only in the quality of a Seleucid official, revocable *ad nutum*.

A few years later (145 B.C.) a new king, Demetrius II., not only recognized the power of Jonathan, but enlarged the territory of Judaea and granted to the Jews, against a lump sum of 300 talents, the exemption from tribute[2] (1 Macc. xi. 34). This was confirmed

---

[1] στρατηγὸς καὶ μεριδάρχης.

[2] If the exemption was complete, how could he write two years later (xiii. 39), ἀφίεμεν τὸν στέφανον ὃν ὀφείλετε? The answer seems to be that all taxes were abolished except the golden crown to be paid upon the investiture of a new

in 143 B.C. when Simon succeeded Jonathan.
Demetrius gave him the titles of high priest
and friend of the King (xiii. 39 ; xiv. 38), and
granted the Jews for ever exemption from
all taxes, even the crown tax. Shortly after,
the Syrian garrison of the citadel of Jerusalem surrendered. In September 141 B.C.,
Simon was solemnly proclaimed perpetual
high priest, general and prince of the Jews [1]
(1 Macc. xiv.).

Lastly, in 139–8 B.C., Demetrius having been
taken prisoner by the Parthians, his brother
Antiochus VI. Sidetes, who was then living
in Rhodes, hurried to assume the crown of
Syria. Even before taking ship, he wrote
to Simon not only to confirm to him all the
privileges granted by his predecessors, and
especially the exemption from tribute, but
also to add, as a supreme gift, the right of
coining money with his own dies (1 Macc.
xv. 5, 6).[2]

---

high priest ; in fact, when Simon succeeded Jonathan he
sent the customary crown to Demetrius (xiii. 37).

[1] ἀρχιερεύς, στρατηγός, ἐθνάρχης.

[2] νῦν οὖν ἵστημί σοι πάντα τὰ ἀφαιρέματα, ἃ ἀφῆκάν σοι
οἱ πρὸ ἐμοῦ βασιλεῖς, καὶ ὅσα ἄλλα δόματα ἀφῆκάν σοι, καὶ

Such being the progress of events, the question arises : What year can be considered as marking the definite emancipation of the Jewish state ?

The first book of Maccabees informs us that when, on the accession of Simon, Demetrius renewed in his favour the privileges granted to Jonathan, and abolished all Seleucid taxes in Judaea, this was the end of the heathen yoke ; in consequence the current year, the 170th of the Seleucid era (143–142 B.C.), was declared " the first of liberty " (1 Macc. xiv. 41–42), and all deeds were henceforth dated by the year of Simon's pontificate. Three years later this computation was still in use, for when Simon's title was proclaimed perpetual, the solemn covenant drawn up on that occasion (172 Seleuc. = 141–140 B.C.) was dated " third year of Simon's pontificate " (1 Macc. xiv. 27).

It seems, however, that even then the attainment of national autonomy was felt to

---

ἐπέτρεψά σοι ποιῆσαι κόμμα ἴδιον νόμισμα τῇ χώρᾳ σου, Ἰερουσαλὴμ δὲ καὶ τὰ ἅγια εἶναι ἐλεύθερα.

be incomplete : a state deprived of the right of coining its own money could not, in the ideas of the ancients, be considered as really autonomous. When, in 139 or 138 B.C., Antiochus VI. gave up this last prerogative, we are led to believe, first, that the Jews had long been requesting the grant ; second, that they hastened to avail themselves of it ; and third, that the political importance of that final victory was well appreciated by them and left some trace in their public documents. Let us see whether such is actually the case.

There exists a remarkable series of heavy silver coins of the Phoenician standard—whole pieces of the weight of 14 grammes, half-pieces of 7 grammes—which have come down to us in a fairly large quantity, especially from two large hoards, found, one in Jerusalem, the other in Jericho. The fabric of these coins is rather thick, not flat and spread like the regal coins of the same standard ; the workmanship is fair, but heavy and sum- mary. The types are, on the obverse a jewelled cup or chalice, on the reverse a

branch of lily with three flowers.[1]  The
legends, written in the old Hebrew character,
commonly but improperly called *Samaritan*,
read :—

*Obverse.*—Shekel Israël (shekel of Israel) ;
(on the half-piece, hatzi ha shekel [*i. e.* half-
shekel]).

*Reverse.* — Yerushalem    ha - Kedoshah [2]
(Jerusalem the holy).   (Plate II. 1, 2.)

Above the reverse type is inscribed a date
expressed by a numeral letter which (except
for year 1) is preceded by the letter *shin*,
initial of *shenath* (year).   The dates go from
1 to 5, but the shekels of the fifth year are
extremely rare and of hasty workmanship ;
and there are no half-shekels of this year.
Some pieces of the years 3 and 4 are in
bronze ; but most likely they were destined
to receive a coating of silver : they are, like so
many pieces of that sort, an official forgery.

That these shekels and half-shekels are a
Jewish currency needs no demonstration, but

---

[1] Earlier numismatists described the types as "a pot
of manna" and "Aaron's rod budding."

[2] On coins of the first year the article is omitted.

there has been much controversy among numismatists as to the precise date to which they belong, opinions varying between the time of Alexander the Great (330 B.C.), nay of Ezra, of Gabinius (57–53 B.C.), and of the first revolt of the Jews against the Romans (66–70 A.D.). However, the majority of scholars since Eckhel agree in attributing them to the time of Simon Maccabaeus, and after duly reconsidering the question, I concur in that doctrine.[1] The chief reasons for not descending so low as the first revolt is the archaic aspect of the coins, their standard (which in 70 A.D. was obsolete, the last Tyrian shekels being of 56 A.D.), the fact that not a single specimen of the shekels ever found was re-struck on a Roman coin, and, lastly, the impossibility of explaining, on this opinion, the existence of shekels of *year 5*; for the revolt cannot really be said

[1] In the first edition of this book I pronounced in favour of the attribution to the first revolt (proposed formerly and briefly by Ewald), and I was followed in this heresy by Imhoof, Babelon, and Kennedy, not always with due acknowledgment of my priority (*e. g.* Kennedy, *loc. cit.* p. 430). However, *dies diem docet.*

to have triumphed before Eloul (September) 66 A.D., and was completely crushed in September 70, lasting therefore only four years.

Now, if we dismiss the time of the first revolt, there is no other period in the history of the Jews before that date that fits exactly the requirements of this coinage, except the time of Simon Maccabaeus and John Hyrcanus. Judaea was then a free state, it had just been authorized to strike money of its own, and by money, in that time, can only be meant silver money—the grant of a bronze currency being too insignificant to be recorded.[1] To be sure, the fabric of our shekels differs widely from that of the Seleucid coins of the period, but the fact is in no way extraordinary. The Jews started a new mint, an entirely new coinage, and it is only natural that they endeavoured to give it a quite peculiar, a national character, as well in its exterior aspect as in its types and legends.

It is to be observed that the dates inscribed

[1] Even under the despot Antiochus IV., Phoenician towns were allowed to coin in bronze.

on the Jewish shekels cannot be counted from
the first year of Simon's pontificate (143–142
B.C.). For, in the first place, Simon could
not possibly, without giving offence, have
struck coins five years before receiving permission to do so ; and secondly, if this was really
the case, we should arrive at the ridiculous
conclusion that Simon left off coining precisely
in the year (sixth year of his pontificate)
when he was allowed to coin ! The inference
is that the era employed on the coins is not
the " era of liberty," beginning 143–142 B.C.,
but what may be termed the " era of full
sovereignty," the origin of which was precisely
the rescript of Antiochus Sidetes granting to
the Jews the crowning privilege of a national
coinage. The substitution of this new era
for the " era of liberty," introduced but a few
years before, is not as astonishing a fact as
might be supposed. Ancient history, nay
Jewish history itself, offers several parallels ;
and even during the French Revolution,
the era of 1789 (first year of liberty) was
promptly superseded by the era of 1792 (first
year of the Republic).

Not only do the Jewish shekels acquaint us with the interesting fact—unknown to historians—that the concession of the right of coinage became the starting-point of a new era in Jerusalem, but they also allow us to settle the date of an important event, the capture of Jerusalem by Antiochus Sidetes.

As is well known from Josephus, the friendly relations between Antiochus and Simon soon came to an end. Simon had been dispensed from the payment of tribute for Judaea and the annexed districts of Samaria, but not for the towns that he had lawlessly occupied outside the boundaries of Judaea proper (Joppa, Gadara), nor for the citadel of Jerusalem. Antiochus having summoned Simon either to pay this tribute or to give up the places in question, Simon refused; so Antiochus repealed all his former concessions [1] and began hostilities (1 Macc. xv. 27). At first they proved unsuccessful, but after Antiochus had crushed his competitor Tryphon and settled the affairs of his realm, he renewed the war against

[1] ἠθέτησε πάντα ὅσα συνέθετο αὐτῷ τὸ πρότερον.

John Hyrcanus, who, in the interval (Feb.
135 B.C.), had succeeded his father Simon.
Jerusalem was besieged, and after an obstinate
resistance, which is commonly believed to
have lasted at least a year,[1] obliged to
capitulate. On the date of these events we
have two conflicting statements. According
to Josephus, the *invasion* of Antiochus took
place "in the fourth year of his reign and the
first of Hyrcanus's," that is, in 136–135 B.C.[2]
So the *siege* may have begun towards August
135, and ended some time after October
134. On the other hand, Porphyrius, in the
Armenian version of Eusebius's Chronicle,

---

[1] For the siege had already lasted some time when
there occurred the heavy rainfalls, δυομένης πλειάδος
(November), and towards the end of it the Feast of
Tabernacles (October) was abolished. (Josephus, xiii.
8, 2.) But see further, p. 18, note.

[2] And not 135–134 B.C. as Schürer puts it (third edition,
i. 259, and so too Bevan, *House of Seleucus*, ii. 239).
The first year of Hyrcanus is certainly 136–135, as Simon
(1 Macc. xvi. 14) was killed in Shebath (February) 177
Sel. = 135 (the Jewish Seleucid year 177 began April 136).
This agrees with the fact that Antiochus's accession
took place in 174 Sel. (1 Macc. xv. 10), viz. 139–138 B.C.
So Antiochus's fourth year is 136–135, identical with
Hyrcanus's first year.

gives as the date of the capture of Jerusalem
the third year of the 162nd Olympiad, viz.
130–129 B.C., and in the text of Josephus
himself we read that the invasion of Antiochus
fell in the second year of that same Olympiad
(131–130), which would give the same year,
130–129, for the surrender of the town. For
intrinsic reasons—a siege of four years being
out of the question—the credibility of this
late date has been often contested, and it has
been suspected that an error of one unit (Ol.
162 instead of 161) has crept into the text of
Eusebius and of Josephus. I think that the
coins allow us to solve the question. If we
admit as probable that the coinage began
in the very year when it was granted, viz.
April 139–138 B.C., then we have the following
concordance :—

Year 1 of the coins. 174 Seleuc. April 139 to April 138[1]
   2  ,,     175  ,,    ,,  138  ,,  137
   3  ,,     176  ,,    ,,  137  ,,  136
   4  ,,     177  ,,    ,,  136  ,,  135
            (February 135, death of Simon).
   5  ,,     178 Seleuc. April 135 to April 134

---

[1] Although in the time of Josephus there were really
two "new years" among the Jews, one for civil purposes

The coins of the first four years belong to Simon, those of the fifth to John Hyrcanus. They are few in number and rude in execution, as may be expected from the circumstances of the war and siege, when they were struck. No coins are known of year 6, viz. after April 134. This proves that the surrender of Jerusalem occurred *at the latest* in the course of that year, and vindicates the first date of Josephus, against his own contradictory statement and the testimony of Porphyrius.[1]

---

in October, one for religious in April, it seems advisable to consider the monetary year, in the time of Simon, as beginning in April, such being undoubtedly the mode of reckoning in the first book of Maccabees.

[1] As Josephus does not give the slightest hint as to the duration of the siege, and even says that on account of the mass of inhabitants provisions speedily grew scanty (§ 240 Niese), it is not impossible that the events recorded by him are not put in a strictly chronological order, so that the Feast of Tabernacles, mentioned § 241, may be *anterior* to the rainfall of November, § 237. I even consider this arrangement as probable, for otherwise the historian ought to have mentioned *two* feasts (October 135 and October 134) instead of one. So I am inclined to adopt the following chronology :—

February 135. Death of Simon. John Hyrcanus accedes.

March 135. Invasion of Antiochus VI.

Summer 135. Antiochus lays waste the country and begins the siege of Jerusalem.

October 135. Feast of Tabernacles.

November ——. Heavy rainfalls.

Before April 134. Surrender of Jerusalem.

## II

In spite of his reputation for mildness and piety which had made him popular with the Jewish people, the conditions imposed by Antiochus Sidetes upon the vanquished Jews were hard enough : their capital was to be dismantled, hostages given, and a heavy tribute paid for the non-Jewish towns left in their possession. To these clauses, mentioned by Josephus, the testimony of the coins allows us to add one that he omits : the right of coining silver was withdrawn from the Jews, or rather, as it had already been snatched from them *inter alia* on the first rupture between Antiochus and Simon, it was not given back to them. If patriotic Jews objected to handle, and especially to use for the Temple fund, coins bearing the effigies of the Seleucid kings, they were soon offered a new alternative. Very few years after the surrender of Jeru-

salem, in 126 B.C., when the civil war was
waging between the sons of Demetrius II.
and the usurper Alexander Zebinas, the
wealthy town of Tyre seems to have snatched
from one of the pretenders to the throne the
practical acknowledgment of its independence
and the right to issue a silver coinage of its
own. The Tyrian coinage, which lasted
for almost two centuries, consists mostly of
shekels (staters), bearing as types the head
of the town god Heracles and the Ptolemaic
eagle ; their legend, "Tyre, the holy and
inviolable," [1] seems to be imitated from the
*Yerushalem Kedoshah* of Simon's shekels
(Pl. II. 3). The dates are reckoned from
the new era of 126 B.C. These coins, not-
withstanding their heathen types and Greek
lettering, were of so exact a weight and so
good an alloy that they enjoyed a large
circulation in Judaea, and were even officially
adopted as "sacred money"; that is to say,
the rabbis decided that the annual head-tax
of one shekel due from every Israelite to the

---

[1] Τύρου ἱερᾶς καὶ ἀσύλου.

Temple treasury was to be paid in *Tyrian money*.[1]

The abolition of the national Jewish coinage was not, however, a complete one. As a sort of crumb of comfort, of little significance, and involving nothing like actual independence, the Jewish high priest was allowed to coin small bronze coins, evidently destined for local circulation only. Although the Seleucid power declined constantly, owing to the advance of the Parthians and Arabs, and the eternal civil strife and general anarchy; although from about 104 B.C. the Hasmonaean high priest took the title of king, at least with regard to his heathen subjects; although under John Hyrcanus (135–104), Judas Aristobulus (104–103), Alexander Jannaeus (103–76) and his widow Queen Alexandra Salome (76–67), the Jewish might expanded in every direction, and grew little by little to a kingdom comparable to that of David and Solomon;—never did the Hasmonaean kings try to revive the regal right of coining

---

[1] Mishna Bekhoroth, viii. 7 ; Tosefta Kebuboth, xii., towards end (undoubtedly after older sources).

silver which Simon and John had enjoyed for a few years. Nay, from 64 B.C., after the Roman suzerainty had succeeded in Syria the Seleucid rule, it seems that even the right of coining bronze was for a time withdrawn from the Jews, for there are no certain coins of the high priest and "ethnarch," John Hyrcanus II. (63–40), and those of the last Hasmonaean, Antigonus (40–37), were struck under the Parthian protectorate and in defiance of the Roman supremacy.

A fairly large number of bronze coins of the Hasmonaeans have been preserved to us. They are of different modules, the largest being the latest. Their types conform scrupulously to Mosaic tradition, and represent none but inanimate objects, for though the Jews did not scruple to make use, even for sacred dues,[1] of coins with figures on them, struck by heathens, they would on the other hand have felt they were transgressing the prohibition of the Deca-

[1] It seems probable, however, that once thrown into the Temple treasury, all gold and silver coins were melted down and transformed into ingots.

logue if they had themselves struck coins of this kind. The types of these bronze coins are rather insignificant, and borrowed for the most part from the contemporary coins of the Ptolemies or the Seleucidae; an olive wreath, a cornucopiae,[1] flower, anchor, star, palm.[2] As to the legends, these fall into two classes. On the most ancient coins, like those of John Hyrcanus I. (Pl. II. 4, 5) and of Judas Aristobulus (Pl. II. 6), as well as on some coins belonging to their successors, the legend is purely Hebrew, and expressed in the following forms: " N . . . (*Jehochanan* or *Jehudah*) *Hakkohen Haggadol Vecheber Hajehudim*," *i. e.* " X . . . High Priest and the Commonwealth of the Jews." We also sometimes find *Rosh Cheber*, " Head of the Commonwealth."

[1] The double cornucopiae is borrowed from the contemporary coins of Alexander Zebinas; it is even possible that some specimens of Hyrcanus's coins are re-struck on Seleucid bronze. The anchor is the well-known badge of the Seleucids.

[2] Some small coins having for type the candlestick with seven branches (Madden, *op. cit.*, p. 102, nos. 8–9) are attributed to the last Hasmonaean Antigonus, but the attribution is anything but certain.

On the more recent coins on the other hand, from Alexander Jannaeus onwards (105–76 B.C.), the legend is often bilingual, Hebrew on one side and Greek on the other. On the one the prince is called by his Jewish name, on the other by a Greek name arbitrarily chosen. Thus Alexander Jannaeus calls himself on one side *Jehonathan Hammelek* (Jonathan the king), on the other βασιλέως Ἀλεξάνδρου (Alexander the king).[1]

Still more curiously the last prince of the dynasty, Antigonus (40–37 B.C.), styles himself high priest on the Hebrew side (*Mattathiah Hakkohen Haggadol, Hacheber Hajehudim*) and king on the Greek side (βασιλέως Ἀντιγόνου). This priest-king reminds us of Maître Jacques in Molière's *Avare*. His coins (Pl. III. 2, 3), which reveal to us his Hebrew name, otherwise unknown to historians, are the only ones of the series

[1] The rare coins of Queen Alexandra, widow and heiress of Alexander Jannaeus, were also probably bilingual, but the Hebrew legend has become illegible. It is known that this queen was called by her Hebrew name Salome (Derenbourg, *Histoire de la Palestine*, p. 102).

which bear regnal dates : these are indicated
by the letter *shin* (the initial letter of *shenath,*
year), followed by an *aleph* (the year 1) or a
*beth* (the year 2).

We see that the legends on the Hasmonaean coins amply confirm the statements of
Josephus as to the history of this dynasty ;
at first scrupulous servants of the theo-
cracy, purely Jews and priests, the de-
scendants of the Maccabees emancipated
themselves little by little from the tutelage
of the Pharisees, entitled themselves kings,
and displayed those very Hellenizing ten-
dencies against which their ancestors had
been the first to revolt. The writing of
these legends is no less interesting than their
contents. These characters have long been
known as the Samaritan alphabet, because
it was believed that the Jews had borrowed
them from their neighbours of Samaria, who
still make use of them. To-day we know
that in reality they represent the primitive
Palestinian form of the Hebrew alphabet.
They approach indeed, with singular close-
ness, to the writing of the most ancient

Hebrew inscriptions—the Stele of Mesha and the inscription of Siloam. This alphabet, consecrated by tradition, remained the only one in use on the purely Jewish coins, even after the square alphabet, coming from Babylon, was introduced into current use: between the coins of Simon or of John Hyrcanus (135 B.C.) and those of Barcochba (135 A.D.) there is no appreciable palaeographical difference.[1]

*It may be asserted that every Jewish coin inscribed in square Hebrew characters is a modern forgery.*

[1] We must renounce the search for a chronological indication in the pointed or round form of the letter *shin*. There are plenty of coins of the time of the Revolts where the *shin* takes the former shape on one side, the latter on the other. On the other hand, the rounded *shin* already figures on the coins of John Hyrcanus, while those of Antigonus have a *shin* resembling a digamma upside down, which is not found anywhere else.

FIG. I.

# III

THE Hasmonaean dynasty ended, like the majority of Oriental dynasties, in bloodshed and imbecility; the last princes of this race were either fierce tyrants like Alexander Jannaeus, or half-idiot high priests like John Hyrcanus II. On two different occasions the civil wars of the Jews necessitated the intervention of the Roman army, which in 64 B.C. had conquered Syria, and superseded the Seleucidae in their capacity of suzerains of the Jews. In 63 B.C., Pompeius, having been chosen to act as arbitrator between the two brothers Hyrcanus and Aristobulus, pronounced in favour of Hyrcanus, and took Jerusalem by assault, its defenders being the partisans of the other pretender. In 37 B.C., C. Sosius, a lieutenant of Marcus Antonius, again conquered Jerusalem, where Antigonus Mattathias, the

28

son of Aristobulus, had established himself with the support of the Parthians. The last scion of the Maccabees was made prisoner, taken to Antioch, and after being flogged was beheaded.

Two curious Roman coins have preserved for us the memory of these events. The first is a silver denarius (Pl. III. 4) bearing the name of Aulus Plautius, who was curule aedile with Plancius in 54 B.C.; this Plautius, an ardent partisan of Pompeius, had probably been one of his lieutenants during his Syrian expedition. On the reverse of his denarius is seen a kneeling figure, with the branch of a suppliant in his hand, and holding a camel by the bridle; around is the legend, *Bacchius Judaeus*. This type is an exact copy of the coins of Scaurus, struck some years before, which commemorated the victory of this general (another of Pompeius's lieutenants) over Aretas, king of Nabathaea; the legend here was *Rex Aretas*. "Bacchius the Jew" may have been some insignificant Syrian prince, more or less Jewish, whose subjection had been the work of Plautius.

Written records make no mention of this
person, but we know that at the time of
Pompeius's expedition there existed in the
Lebanon district several rulers of this kind,
holding a position midway between that of
brigand chief and of king. One of these,
mentioned by Josephus,[1] was called *Dionysios;*
is it not possible that Bacchius is simply the
Latin translation of this Greek name?[2]

The bronze coin of Sosius (Pl. III. 5) is
yet more interesting, for it served as the
prototype of the famous coins of Vespasian
with the legend *Judaea capta.* The reverse
represents a trophy erected between a Jewish
prisoner in bonds (possibly meant for Antigonus) and a Jewish female captive, a per-
sonification of Judaea. Around is the name
of the conqueror: *C. Sosius imp(erator).* On
the obverse of the coin is the portrait of
Antonius, and the letters *Za*, the initials of

---

[1] Josephus, *Ant.* xiv. 3, 2.   He was tyrant of Tripolis.
His neighbour Silas was expressly designated as a Jew.

[2] The opinion that Bacchius the Jew is Aristobulus,
priest of the (Jewish) Bacchus (*i.e.* Jehovah), is very
unlikely.

the word *Zacynthus*, the island in which this bronze coin was struck.

In the place of the Hasmonaeans, who were extinct in the male line, the Romans put upon the throne of Judaea the Idumaean Herod, whose father Antipater had already been Mayor of the Palace in the reign of Hyrcanus II. Herod reigned thirty-three years, and proved a despot, active, cruel and ostentatious. From the political point of view, he showed himself the very docile vassal of Rome. Like the majority of other vassal princes, he was only authorized to strike bronze coins. Although but little inclined to follow the traditions of the Pharisees, and probably believing but little himself, Herod respected the national sentiment in the choice of his monetary types; he represented only inanimate objects, some (Pl. IV. 1) borrowed from the Hasmonaean bronze coins (the palm, crown, cornucopiae), while others were new (tripod, helmet, *acrostolion*), sometimes laying claim to a Macedonian origin (the Macedonian shield). The most remarkable pieces (Pl III. 6) are

those which bear a regnal date expressed
in the Egyptian fashion by the sign **LГ** (the
year three) and a monogram, which is a
mark showing the value (the initial letters
of the word τρίχαλκον).　On all these coins,
as on those of the other princes of the
Idumaean dynasty, the legend is purely
Greek : βασιλέως Ἡρώδου, " King Herod "
(we know that from the time of Herod
onwards the functions of king and high
priest were kept strictly separate).　The
exclusive employment of the Greek language
proves how widely the knowledge of this
tongue had spread among the Jews.

Towards the end of his life, Herod seems
to have departed from his habitual display of
consideration for the religious feelings or
prejudices of his subjects.　He planted a
gold eagle on the pediment of the Temple of
Jehovah, and a few days before his death he
suppressed, not without bloodshed, a revolt
which this heathen symbol had provoked.
To this troubled period are attributed some
small bronze coins, on the reverse of which is
represented an eagle.　(Fig. 1, p. 28.)

On the death of Herod, his dominions were divided between his sons, who had to content themselves with the more modest titles of *tetrarch* and *ethnarch*. Herod Philip reigned over the territories to the east and north-east (Batanaea, Trachonitis, and Hauran), on the borders of the desert; Herod Antipas had Galilee and Peraea; Judaea properly so called was assigned to the eldest son, Herod Archelaus. The first two princes reigned for long periods; their coins are of small interest, and do not, properly speaking, belong to Jewish numismatics. All have regnal dates or Greek legends: " Herod (or Philip), tetrarch," on one side, the name of the reigning emperor on the other.[1] As to types, the bronze coins of Antipas (Pl. IV. 2) have the palm and the wreath. Those of Philip (Pl. IV. 3), which were struck in a country where the Jewish population was in a minority, broke away from the observance of the command in the Decalogue concerning the representation of animate objects: they ex-

[1] On some coins of Antipas (Pl. IV. 2) the name of the emperor is replaced by that of the capital (Tiberias).

hibit on one side the head of the emperor,
and on the other a tetrastyle temple, which
was doubtless the temple of Augustus, built
by Herod the Great in the city of Caesarea-
Paneas, where Philip resided.

To return to Jerusalem. Herod Archelaus,
the son of Herod the Great, there struck coins
of bronze, resembling those of his father,
with the Greek legend, " Herod Ethnarch,"
and bearing types as numerous as they are
unimportant [1] (Pl. IV. 4). At the end of ten
years this brutal tyrant had made himself so
unpopular that the Jewish notables demanded
and obtained his deposition ; Archelaus was
exiled to Vienne in Gaul, and Judaea was
reduced to a province (6 A.D.), or rather to a
dependency of the province of Syria. Nevertheless, the Idumaean dynasty was still to
furnish Judaea with a sovereign. Thirty
years after the deposition of Archelaus,
Agrippa, one of Herod's grandsons, who had
been brought up in Rome and had succeeded
in ingratiating himself with Caligula, received

[1] Bunch of grapes, helmet, caduceus, anchor, prow,
cornucopiae, wreath, and galley.

from the latter the tetrarchies of Antipas and Philip, which had become vacant by the death or the exile of their rulers (37–40 A.D.). After the death of Caligula and the elevation of Claudius to the supreme power, Agrippa, who had contributed to this result, received in addition Judaea itself. He then united under his sceptre all the possessions of his grandfather, and was authorized to assume the title of king. This hoary libertine was a king after the heart of the Pharisees. His Jewish coins, properly so called, present (Pl. IV. 5, 6) on the obverse the singular type of an umbrella, which has also been taken for a tabernacle; on the reverse, three ears of corn, the emblem of prosperity. His name he gives in Greek as King Agrippa, and marks the coins with a regnal date, always the year 6.

Besides these coins, which were intended for circulation in a Jewish country, Agrippa struck some much less orthodox pieces, on which figured some quite pagan types (Victory, Fortune, etc.), the portrait of the reigning emperor, and sometimes even that of

Agrippa himself and his son on horseback.
On some, as on his inscriptions on stone, he
takes the ostentatious title of "The great
King Agrippa, the friend of Caesar" (βασι-
λεὺς μέγας Ἀγρίππας φιλόκαισαρ). These
coins were doubtless intended to circulate
only in Agrippa's old tetrarchies, or in the
towns on the sea-coast, where there was a very
mixed population; the majority, indeed, bear
the name of a new city, Caesarea or Tiberias.

Finally, a third type is represented by a
very singular issue, which appears to be less
a coin properly so called than a medal commemorating the accession of Agrippa and his
alliance with the Romans, which had most
likely been officially inscribed on a bronze
tablet in Rome, as was the custom. It dis-
plays on one side, "King Agrippa, the friend
of Caesar"; on the other, two hands clasped
surrounded by a wreath—the emblem of a
treaty of alliance—and a long inscription:
"Friendship and alliance of King Agrippa
with the Senate and the People of Rome."

Agrippa I. only reigned four years in
Judaea. On his death (44 A.D.) his kingdom

was for a second time reduced to the status of Roman provincial territory. Judaea properly so called never again changed its political condition. As to the other territories—the tetrarchies of Antipas and of Philip—they were once more constituted a principality in the interest of Agrippa's son, Agrippa II. (the brother of the famous Berenice), whose life was prolonged till at least 95 A.D.[1] But although Agrippa II. was an Israelite and retained some of his rights over Jerusalem, notably that of living in the palace of the Herods, and of nominating the high priest, his coinage, like his policy, had nothing national about it, and it is only by straining the sense of the words that his coins can be reckoned among Jewish coins.[2]

---

[1] Indeed Photius (cod. 33) makes him live till 100 A.D., but this information has often been suspected, and it seems difficult to admit that Josephus's *Vita*, where Agrippa is mentioned as dead (c. 65), was written so late. The last dated coins are of the year 35 = 95 A.D.

[2] The coins of Agrippa II. are either *autonomous* or *imperial*, but in neither case do they conform to the Jewish law. The former have on the obverse the head of Agrippa, a hand holding ears of corn, or a head

It is just the same in the case of the contemporary coins of the "Kingdom" of Chalcis in Lebanon, which was ruled over by a collateral branch of the family of the Herods.[1]

(Tyche) with a turreted crown; the latter (Pl. IV. 7) bear the head of the reigning emperor, with his titles (often very incorrectly expressed) in Greek or Latin. On the reverse the types are various, but without interest (Fortune, Victory, galley, wreath, palm, altar, cornucopiae and caduceus, anchor, circle). There exist, besides, the municipal coins of Caesarea Philippi (now called Neronias) and of Tiberias, which bear the name of Agrippa: the coins of this prince are all dated, mostly by an era beginning 61 A.D., which may be the local era of Neronias. Some coins mention another era five years older.

[1] Herod I., brother of Agrippa I. (41–48 A.D.); his son Aristobulus and Queen Salome (Babelon, *Revue numismatique*, 1883, p. 145; Imhoof, *Porträtköpfe*, vi. 21, 22).

# IV

WE have seen that on two different occasions—after the deposition of Archelaus, and again on the death of Agrippa I.—Judaea was reduced to the position of a provincial territory by the Romans. This territory, which had Caesarea for its capital, was governed by an official of somewhat inferior rank, the procurator, who, from the military point of view, was subordinate to the governor of Syria. The gold and silver coins of Rome gradually supplanted at this time the Greek money of preceding periods. We still (until about 56 A.D.) have to deal with the Tyrian staters—which were especially appropriated to the payment of religious taxes—but the coins most current in Syria were the Graeco-Roman tetradrachms of Antioch and the Roman denarius, which had been made legally equivalent to the Attic drachm. It

was a coin of this kind (Pl. V. 1) which the
Pharisees and the Herodians, *i. e.* the partisans of the theocratic republic on the one
hand, and of the Idumaean dynasty on the
other, showed to Christ when they asked
Him whether it were lawful to pay tribute.
"Whose is this image and superscription?"
He asked them. They replied, "Caesar's."
"Render therefore unto Caesar the things
which are Caesar's; and unto God the things
that are God's." [1]

Besides these silver denarii, Judaea also
possessed a bronze coinage of lower de-
nomination, issued by the procurators in
imitation of the Hasmonaean and Idumaean
princes. These coins were not struck under
the authority of the Senate, like the ordinary
Roman brass; Judaea being considered as an
imperial district, they bear the name of the
reigning emperor in Greek. There was also
sometimes associated with this, or substi-
tuted for it, the name of the emperor's
mother, or of his son; they also bear a

[1] St. Matt. xxii. 15 ff.

regnal date. These coins[1] circulated only
in Judaea, and were probably struck by
Jewish workmen; this is doubtless the
reason why the procurators represented on
them only inanimate objects (Pl. V. 3), in
conformity with the Mosaic law (ear of corn,
palm-tree or branch, cornucopiae, *diota*,
covered vase, wreath, etc.). We repro-
duce here (Pl. V. 2) a coin of the procurator
Pontius Pilate, struck in the year of the
Crucifixion (the eighteenth year of Tiberius,
35 A.D.). The types are the laurel-wreath
and the *lituus* or augur's wand.

If the procurators had shown as much
tolerance in the rest of their administration
as in their coinage, Judaea would easily have
resigned herself to the loss of her independence. But numerous tactless blunders, sometimes even real acts of persecution, wounded
the religious sentiment of the people; the
avarice or the injustice of certain governors
completed the exasperation of the Jews, who

---

[1] They may be termed *quadrantes*, a name twice used
in the New Testament. Their legal value was the fourth
of an *as*.

were already greatly excited by party spirit
and the ebullition of feeling due to Messianic
expectations. The tyranny of the governors
increased in the same proportion as the
fanaticism of their subjects. But at last a
day came when the cup was full to over-
flowing, and the revolt of despair broke out :
it was accompanied by deplorable excesses,
but Tacitus himself recognized that the
responsibility for the first wrongs lay with
the Romans. *Duravit patientia Judaeis
usque ad Gessium Florum. . .*[1]

The revolution really triumphed in *Eloul*
(September) 66 A.D., the date on which the
Roman garrison of the castle in Jerusalem
capitulated. It ended on *Eloul* (September)
8th, 70 A.D., the date on which the last
quarters of the city were retaken by the
soldiers of Titus.[2] It lasted, therefore,
almost exactly four Jewish years. In this
interval the Jews were masters of the whole
of Palestine (Judaea, Samaria, and Galilee)

[1] Tacitus, *Hist.* v. 10.
[2] *Ibid.* vi. 8, 5. The Temple is known to have been
burnt on *Ab* (August) 10th, and not 9th (*Ibid.* vi. 4, 5).

until the end of 67 A.D., of a part of Judaea until the middle of 69, of Jerusalem alone and some of the lesser strongholds during the last year.

The numismatic records of the great Jewish rebellion are singularly few and unimportant in number. They consist chiefly of small bronze coins, whose types are a vine- (or fig-) leaf and a two-handled vase, with or without a lid (Pl. V. 4). The legend reads : obverse, *Cheruth Zion* (liberty of Zion); reverse, *Shenath Shetaim* (year 2) or *Shalosh* (3). So we have here a new monetary era, starting, as it seems, from September 66 A.D., for in those days the civil year undoubtedly began in autumn.

In the fourth year other bronze coins were struck, some of them of a larger module. Their types are (Pl. V. 5, 6), on one side the citron (*ethrog*) between the two bundles of twigs (*lulab*) which the Jews carried in the Feast of Tabernacles ; on the other side sometimes a cup, sometimes a palm-tree between two baskets. The legend is uniformly *Ligullath Zion* (deliverance of Zion), the date

*Shenath arba* (year 4). Moreover, the larger
coins bear a mark of value *chatzi* (half) ;
the middle-sized *rebra* (quarter). What the
unit was, of which these are the fractions, is
not clear. I am inclined to think that it was
the shekel. At any rate, we have here not
an ordinary divisional coinage, but a sort of
obsidional money, a money of necessity,
forcibly introduced into currency with a
nominal value far above its intrinsic worth ;
in fact, the equivalent of modern paper
money offered by bankrupt states. The
circumstances will explain this exceptional
coinage ; "year 4" corresponds to Sept. 69—
Sept. 70 A.D., the period when the Jewish
rebellion was restricted to Jerusalem, then
closely besieged by the Romans, and when
most likely all the reserve of silver and
gold, formerly hoarded in the treasury of the
Temple, had been exhausted by the necessities
of war. The bronze coinage formed a tem-
porary substitute for the normal currency.

FIG. 2.

## V.

AFTER lasting for four years the Jewish revolt was quenched in streams of blood. Not only was the independence of Israel no longer in question, but Palestine had now become a special province occupied by a Roman legion (the Tenth *Fretensis*, of which some coins still remain) ; the holy city and the Temple, destroyed by fire, lay in ruins. The Romans celebrated their victory, so dearly bought, by the erection of the Arch of Titus, and by numerous coins of every kind of metal and of every module, the types of which bear reference to the suppression of the Jewish revolt. These coins, struck in the name of the emperors Vespasian, Titus, and Domitian, and bearing their effigies, belong to a well-known class, of which the money of Sosius, mentioned above, which commemorated the defeat of the last

45

of the Maccabees, is one of the earliest examples. The most ordinary type represents a captive—Judaea—seated or standing at the foot of a palm-tree or a trophy. On the other side of this central *motif* is represented sometimes, as on the coins of Sosius, a Jewish prisoner, sometimes (Pl. VI. 1) the victorious emperor in military attire. In another group of coins the type is a Victory inscribing the name of the emperor on a shield, which she supports against a palm-tree (Pl. VI. 3). The legend, *Judaea devicta* (Pl. VI. 2), on the gold and silver coins (sometimes in Greek : ΙΟΥΔΑΙΑΣ ΕΑΛΩΚΥΙΑΣ)—*Judaea capta* on the bronze —leaves no doubt as to the interpretation of these sufficiently transparent symbols.

In the interval of sixty years which separates the two revolts, we find, further, two Roman coins, which are closely bound up with Jewish history. One is the large bronze coin (Pl. VII. 1) of Nerva (96–98), the reverse of which gives a representation of a palm-tree, with the legend, *Fisci· Judaici calumnia sublata* (the suppression of the prosecutions in connection with the Jewish treasury). The *fiscus Judaicus* was simply the poll-tax of the half-shekel (or the di-drachm) formerly paid by all the faithful to the Temple at Jerusalem, to which the Romans, now that the Temple no longer existed, laid claim, to their own profit. The Jews naturally abhorred this impious tax, the proceeds of which were cast into the treasury of Jupiter Capitolinus at Rome; hence they strove to conceal their Israelite origin, in order to be exempt from payment. These dissimulations brought in their train accusations, vexatious prosecutions, and visits which were something more than domiciliary. The bronze coin of Nerva, which belongs to a period of comparative pacification, commemorates the suppression of these abuses (*calumnia*), though not of the tax itself.

The bronze coin of Hadrian (Pl. VII. 2), struck in his third consulate (130 A.D.), is no less curious. It is a souvenir of a journey which this nomad emperor made in Judaea, and of the official cordiality with which he was

received.  On it we see Judaea, followed by
her children, advancing towards Hadrian
with a patera in her hand to offer a
libation on the altar from which the flame
already rises; behind her walks a bull, the
victim appointed for the sacrifice.  Legend,
*Adventui Aug. Iudaeae.*

These imperial visits, this enthusiasm
procured to order, marked the calm that
preceded the storm.  Already, at the end of
Trajan's reign, a bloody insurrection had
broken out among the Jewish colonies
of Mesopotamia, Cyprus, Egypt, and the
Cyrenaïca.  As a consequence of Hadrian's
tour and of acts of provocation, the details
of which are but little known, the Jews
in Palestine took up arms in their turn
(133 A.D.).  The revolt was protracted and
desperate.  It had at its head an adventurer
named in Jewish documents Bar Koziba, in
Christian documents *Bar Cochba*, "the son
of the star," doubtless an allusion to the
prophecy of Balaam : "There shall come a
star out of Jacob, and a sceptre shall rise out
of Israel, and shall smite the corners of

Moab, and destroy all the children of Sheth."
Barcochba passed himself off, indeed, as the
Messiah, and he was recognized as such by
the learned doctor Akiba. This man and
another rabbi, Eleazar of Modein, the uncle
of Barcochba, whom his nephew ended by
suspecting of treason and kicked to death,
were the only notable doctors who sided
with the insurgents; the rest of the rabbis
stood aside. The rebels, who reached the
number of 200,000, after having occupied
several strongholds and probably Jerusalem
itself, were hunted from one shelter to
another, and were finally exterminated in the
fortress of Bethar, their last refuge (135 A.D.).

Like their predecessors, the insurgents of
66 A.D., the rebels under Hadrian asserted
the independence of Judaea by striking coins;
but their insurrection was of a very different
character from the first, and this difference
finds expression in the types and legends of
the coins.

The insurgents of 66 were enthusiastic
Pharisees (zealots), jealous democrats, un-
disciplined, and levelling all distinctions;

E

hence their coins bore no proper name. *Tres duces, tot exercitus*, said Tacitus ; the partisans of Eleazar, the son of Simon, would have refused to use the coins of Simon Bargioras, while those of Bargioras would have had none of John of Giscala's. The sacred name of Jerusalem brought every one into agreement. On the other hand, Barcochba seems to have been, at least in the last years, absolute dictator ; he clearly aimed at kingship, and as his uncle, Eleazar, was a native of Modein, the country of the Maccabees, it is by no means impossible that Barcochba was connected by birth with the royal family of the Hasmonaeans.[1] Hence he caused his own name to appear on the great majority of his coins ; but this name is not the patronymic or punning name given him by Christian or Talmudic texts, but the name of *Simon*, our knowledge of which comes from the coins alone. We need not

[1] In the unintelligible text of Syncellus (p. 660, 18 : Χοχεβᾶς τις ὁ μονογενὴς (only son ?) ἡγεῖτο), is it possible that the word Ἀσαμωνογενὴς, *descendant of the Hasmonaeans*, is concealed ?

be greatly astonished that it has not been
handed down by the written documents, for
we know from other examples that persons
who bore very common names were habit-
ually designated by their patronymics in
order to avoid confusion. So in the first
insurrection Simon Bargioras is called by
Dion Cassius simply Bargioras, and Tacitus
even gives him in error the *praenomen* of
John.[1]

In the time of Barcochba the Temple and
its treasure existed no longer ; so there were
no gold or silver ingots to be got from which
the insurgents could have manufactured the
blanks of their coins. On the other hand, the
autonomous money of Tyre, formerly accepted even for sacred purposes, had ceased to
be struck since about 56 A.D. and was becoming scarce. No other silver was therefore to
be had than the Graeco-Roman tetradrachms
issued by the imperial mint of Antioch, and
perhaps that of Tyre, for the use of the
Greek-speaking Eastern provinces, and the
Roman denarii. These were the coins used

[1] Tacit., *Hist.* v. 12 ; Dion, xvi. 7.

by the insurgents, but in their fanatic hatred
of a foreign yoke and of the Greek civilization,
they re-struck them with dies orthodox in
their design, in order to obliterate the abhorred
types and inscriptions of their masters. All
the smaller silver coins of Barcochba are
Roman denarii (*cp.* Pl. VIII. 1) or Graeco-
Roman drachms of Caesarea in Cappadocia
re-struck with Jewish types, and the re-striking was sometimes so hasty that the old
legend, and sometimes the old head, are still
visible at the edge of the blank. There are
even coins on which it has been possible to
decipher the names of the Roman emperors
posterior to the first revolt (from Galba to
Hadrian), and this has allowed us to attribute
with certainty to Barcochba the denarii with
the name of Simon. It follows that the
coins on which the re-striking is not apparent,
as they have exactly the weight, the types,
and the legends of the others, belong to the
same period and are themselves only denarii,
re-struck, but with greater care.[1]

[1] See Hamburger, *Die Münzprägungen während des
letzten Aufstandes der Israeliten gegen Rom,* 1892.

These general observations make it possible
for me to be very brief in the enumeration
of the monetary types of Barcochba. His
coinage comprises pieces of silver and of
bronze. The former are, first of all, the re-
struck Roman denarii which we have just
been discussing (Pl. VIII. 2–5). The types
are, on the obverse, the crown (Pl. VIII. 4) or
the bunch of grapes (Pl. VIII. 3, 5); on the
reverse, a vase and a palm-branch (Pl. VIII.
4), a palm-branch alone (Pl. VIII. 2), a lyre
(Pl. VIII. 5), or two trumpets (Pl. VIII. 3,
sacred instruments, which are thus represented on the Arch of Titus). The legend on
the obverse is invariably *Simon* (the name
sometimes spelt in a curious fashion); on the
reverse, *Sh*(enath) *beth lecher*(uth) *Israel*,
"year 2 of the liberty of Israel," or simply
*Lecheruth Yerushalem*, "liberty of Jerusalem"
—a new era of liberty, the third we have
met with in Jewish numismatics. The coins
with this latter inscription, which do not differ
in any way from the others, appear to have
been struck in Jerusalem, and thus confirm the
indication, furnished by several texts, that the

insurgents were for some time masters of the ruins of this city.

Parallel to these re-struck denarii exists a series of " shekels," or rather debased Attic tetradrachms (Pl. VIII. 6), the bulk, if not the whole, of which have been re-struck on imperial tetradrachms of Antioch, mostly of the reign of Trajan. Their obverse type is a portico with four columns, *i.e.* a conventional representation of the Temple at Jerusalem, which the insurgents proposed to rebuild. Above the Temple is usually an adjunct symbol, a star—perhaps an allusion to the name Barcochba, "son of the star"—which sometimes appears degraded as a cross. The type of the reverse—*ethrog* and *lulab*, or *lulab* alone—recalls the analogous types of the first rebellion. The tetradrachms of the first year (*shenath achath ligullath Israel*, " year 1 of the deliverance of Israel") bear on the obverse the name of *Jerusalem*; those of the second year (*sh*(enath) *beth lecher*(uth) *Israel*, "year 2 of the liberty of Israel") bear sometimes the name of *Jerusalem*, sometimes the name of *Simon*; the

undated coins (*lecheruth Yerushalem*, "liberty
of Jeusalem ") bear only this latter name.

As the reader will observe, there exist no
*silver* coins of the first year of the rebellion—
either denarii or tetradrachms—with the name
of Simon. Who was, then, the head of the new
commonwealth during that year? The reply
to this question has been supplied by the
discovery of a curious coin, the only known
specimen of which (Fig. 2, p. 45) belongs to the
cabinet of the Marquis de Vogüé in Paris. It is
a re-struck denarius, having as types on one
side a vase and palm, on the other a bunch of
grapes. The legend runs on the obverse,
*Eleazar hakkohen* (Eleazar the priest); on the
reverse, *Shenath achath ligullath Israël*, "year
1 of the deliverance of Israel." That this
Eleazar (whose bronze coins will be mentioned
presently) is a contemporary of Simon Barcochba appears from several " hybrid" specimens of re-struck denarii, which exhibit
simultaneously on one side the die (obverse or reverse) of Eleazar, on the other
the die of Simon. But the historical identification of the "priest Eleazar" remains

quite uncertain. Some believe him to be
identical with the rabbi Eleazar (or rather
Elieser) of Modein, uncle and victim of
Barcochba, who, however, is not reported to
have been a priest; others have proposed
Eleazar ben Azaria, who, in fact, was of
priestly descent, or Eleazar ben Harsom.

In addition to the silver coinage, the insurgents under Hadrian struck, or rather re-struck,
a great many bronze coins of various sizes.
Some are dated from the first year of the
deliverance of Israel (*shenath achath ligullath
Israël*) or from the second (*sh. beth lecheruth Israël*); others bear simply the lettering,
*lecheruth Yerushalem*, "liberty of Jerusalem."
Among the bronze coins of year 1, a few are
struck in the name of the priest Eleazar
(*Eleazar hakkohen*); their types are a palm-
tree and a bunch of grapes (Pl. IX. 1). Other
coins of the same year, some of which are of
very large size, bear the legend *Simon Nasi
Israël*, "Simon prince of Israel" (types: wreath
and two-handled vase (Pl. IX. 2), palm-tree
and vine-leaf; wreath, palm-branch and lyre).
Although the title *nasi* was used in later years

to designate the president of the rabbinic
Sanhedrin, it seems probable that it is employed here in a profane sense, and that
"Simon Nasi" is no other than Simon Barcochba. In the year 2 the name of Eleazar
disappears; but there are a few coins of Simon,
with the simple legend *Simon* and the same
types as in year 1 (Pl. IX. 3); on some rare
specimens (type: palm-tree and cluster of
grapes) the legend, instead of Simon, reads
*Yerushalem*. The bronze coins without a
date exhibit the same varieties as those of
the year 2.

I am unwilling to leave the coins of the
second Jewish revolt without mentioning the
allusion made to the subject in a well-known
passage of the Talmud. "The *Ma'aser Sheni*"
(the second tithe), say the rabbis, "cannot be
paid in a coinage which is not current, like
the coins of Koziba or of Jerusalem, or that
of the former kings.[1]"

---

[1] Toseſta, *Ma'aser Sheni*, I. 5. The same passage is
reproduced with alterations in the Talmud of Jerusalem
(*Ma'aser Sheni*, I. 2) and in that of Babylon (*Baba Kamma*,
97 *b*). The coins of the revolts are here classed together

The coins of Koziba are the tetradrachms
and denarii of Simon Barcochba, whom the
rabbis, his enemies, often call *Ben Koziba*,
"the son of the lie." The coins of Jerusalem are the tetradrachms of the second
revolt, with the legend "Jerusalem." The
"coins of the former kings" are the shekels
and half-shekels of Simon the Hasmonaean,
perhaps also the tetradrachms of the Seleucidae and the Ptolemies, which were no
longer current at the time when the *halakha*
was drawn up.

---

under the common heading, "Money of the time of
danger," and the Rabbi Ime decides that they ought to
be cast into the sea.

# VI

WITH the coins of Barcochba we have finished our excursion across the domain of Jewish numismatics. While the first revolt had as its consequence the destruction of the Temple, the second brought in its train the almost complete extermination of the Jewish population of Palestine. Numbers of heathen colonists took the place of the old inhabitants, and on the site of Jerusalem there arose a Roman town called Aelia Capitolina, after the Emperor Aelius Hadrian and Jupiter Capitolinus, whose temple replaced that of Jehovah. This town, which the Jews were forbidden to enter, held the rank of a colony, and has left a long series of bronze coins, which extends from Hadrian to Valerian (136–260 A.D.). The two most interesting types are reproduced here. One represents the foundation of the city—a colonist draw-

ing the furrow to mark the limits of the
future enclosure (Pl. X. 1). The other shows
the three divinities—Jupiter, Juno, and
Minerva—who were worshipped in the
temple of Jupiter Capitolinus at Rome and
at Aelia (Pl. X. 2).

Jerusalem is not the only city in Palestine
in which the pagan worship took possession
of places formerly devoted to the worship of
the true God. The famous temple of the
Samaritans on Mount Gerizim, which had
already once before been transformed into
a temple of Zeus Xenios, and then was
restored to monotheistic worship, had been
disestablished a second time in favour of
Jupiter. This temple is represented on a
very picturesque coin of Neapolis (the new
capital of Samaria, the present Nablous)
struck under the Emperor Antoninus Pius
(Pl. X. 3).

Nevertheless, at the time when Judaism
was being thus humiliated, hunted and
exterminated in its native country, it found
a source of strength even in its defeat, expanded more and more in the countries of

the dispersion, and gained dominion over the souls of many. Not only did Jewish monotheism and Jewish morality gain proselytes up to the very steps of the throne, but the heathen legends began to reconcile themselves with Jewish traditions, and to merge themselves into them. We have a very remarkable example of this gradual fusion on a coin of Apamea in Phrygia, which dates from the reign of the Emperor Septimius Severus, and was repeated several times under the following reigns (Pl. XI.). On the reverse of this coin are seen two figures, a man and woman, seated in a chest, floating on the water ; on the open lid is perched a bird. On the left is another scene, which continues the first in order of time ; the two people have left the chest, and the bird is bringing them an olive branch. In this description will be recognized without difficulty a well-known episode in the history of the Deluge. Traditions analogous to those of the Bible existed among the heathen : the Phrygians in particular had their myth about the Deluge, which in the end became localized

at Apamea Cibotus, Apamea "the Chest."
As this town, from the time of Cicero[1]
onwards, contained a large Jewish population, a fusion of the two legends must have
been effected at an early period. We find a
proof of this elsewhere in a passage in the
Sibylline Books, where the writer recounts
how the ark of Noah came to a standstill at
the source of the river Marsyas, *i. e.* near
Apamea Cibotus.[2] Now imagine a Judaizing,
or, say, well-read magistrate of Apamea, at
the end of the second century—the "agono-
thetes," or aedile, Artemas—charged with the
invention of a new type for the coins of this
town. It will be understood how he would
hasten to make choice of one which had the
singular merit of reconciling in the happiest

---

[1] See Cicero, *pro Flacco*, 28. The quantity of gold
(destined for the Temple at Jerusalem) confiscated by
Flaccus from the Jews at Apamea was valued at a hundred
pounds, an amount which, given the relative value of
gold and of silver, corresponds to about 330 kilogrammes
of silver, or 37,500 half-shekels, a quantity so consider-
able that it must represent the contribution of several
years or some extraordinary gifts.

[2] *Libri Sibyllini*, i. 273.

manner the Hebrew traditions with those of the locality; moreover, to remove any shadow of doubt, it was Noah's name (ΝΩΕ) which he had engraved in full on the ark; the deluge of Apamea and the deluge of Noah are truly, for him, one and the same.

Let us conclude with this example, both piquant and consoling, of a religious syncretism, which was at that time visible in some degree throughout the heathen world to the profit of Judaism and its first-born, Christianity. It is the time when the unknown author of the Treatise on the Sublime does not fear to borrow an example of "sublime" literature from the Book of Genesis; it is the time when the Emperor Severus Alexander placed in his oratory a bust of Orpheus between busts of Abraham and of Christ. Two centuries later, and a poet, a pagan fanatic, cried with an indignation which bears witness to his sincerity : [1]

Atque utinam nunquam Judaea subacta fuisset
Pompeii bellis imperioque Titi!
Latius excisae pestis contagia serpunt
Victoresque suos natio victa premit.

---

[1] Rutilius Namatianus, *Itinera*, v. 385.

FIG. 3.

# APPENDIX

### FALSE SHEKELS.[1]

EVERY numismatist is familiar with the
pieces, generally roughly cast in more or less
poor silver, which are passed off as genuine
Jewish shekels (Fig. 3). The inscriptions are
the same as those which we find on the
genuine coins, except that they are in modern
Hebrew letters, and that no date is given.
The types approximate to those of the true
coin ; but instead of the lily with three
flowers we have a branch with many leaves ;
and the chalice is replaced by an object
apparently meant, to judge by the fumes

[1] This appendix is extracted, with the permission of
Messrs. Bemrose and Sons, from an article in the
*Reliquary and Illustrated Archæologist* for October 1902.

arising from it, for a pot full of incense. No one who has seen the genuine struck shekel could for a moment be deceived by this cast piece. Nevertheless, so few people take the trouble to test the truth of what is told them about Biblical antiquities, that tradesmen find it worth their while to offer for sale facsimiles of these impostures. Before me is an atrociously badly cast facsimile which is sold by one of the largest firms of general dealers in London, together with the following printed description :—

### CAST-IRON MODEL OF JEWISH SHEKEL.

This is a facsimile of a genuine Shekel (called in the Bible " a piece of silver "), coined by Simon Maccabaeus, who was King of the Jews, 172–142 B.C.

It was issued in the year 170 B.C. It is, therefore, now 2,068 years old.

For thirty " pieces of silver " Judas betrayed our Lord. The Hebrew inscriptions on the obverse and reverse mean "Shekel of Israel" and " Liberator of Jerusalem," and the designs represent the pot of manna and Aaron's rod that budded.

Quite apart from the initial error of supposing the original of this facsimile to be a genuine Jewish shekel, this short paragraph

F

is well worth study for the other misrepre-
sentations compressed into it.   The date of
Simon's election to the leadership of the Jews
is generally supposed to be 143–142 B.C.
Unless, therefore, the worthy person who
compiled the paper has other information, I am
inclined to think that he has been misled by
some comparative table of eras, in which the
Seleucid year 170 corresponds to the year
143–142 B.C.   It would be interesting to know
how he ascertains the exact year in which the
coin was issued, since it bears no regnal date.
The translation, " Liberator of Jerusalem," is
also new, and may have been suggested by
the legend, " Deliverance of Zion," found on
some other Jewish coins.   At the end of all
this it would have been surprising indeed to
miss the identification of the types as the pot
of manna and Aaron's rod that budded.[1]
The implication that the "thirty pieces of
silver " were of this kind was also inevitable ;
but the history of this matter would require a
chapter to itself.

[1] This is the traditional but unfounded explanation of
the types of the true shekel.

M. A. Levy, in his *Jüdische Münzen*
(1862), p. 163, says that the commonest of
the forgeries of the Jewish shekel is a piece
exactly corresponding to the one we have
described. He mentions other forgeries,[1] but
we may for the present confine ourselves to
this, the most important—that is, the one
which has made most victims. How far can
we trace it back? We find it in Erasmus
Froelich's *Annales Regum et Rerum Syriae*
(Vienna, 1754) illustrated on Pl. XIX. (No. v.)
among the "modern Hebrew coins," which
he gives as a warning to collectors. He says
(*Prolegomena*, p. 92) that he has seen many
specimens, varying in metal, weight, etc., but
all manifestly false and modern. He sup-
poses that they are due to an unsuccessful
attempt to imitate the true shekels. In J.
Leusden's *Philologus Hebraeo-mixtus* (4th
ed., 1739, p. 207) it is also illustrated, this
time as a genuine shekel; the types are ex-
plained as an incense-cup and Aaron's rod;

[1] The section of Levy's work relating to forgeries of
Jewish coins is translated at length by Madden, *Coins of
the Jews* (1881), pp. 314 f.

and the branch is represented as if it were growing up out of a mound.

The work of Caspar Waser, *de antiquis numis Hebraeorum*, etc., Zürich, 1605, was known to Leusden. It is surprising, therefore, that the genuine shekel, which is moderately well represented by Waser (pp. 59 f.), should be ignored by the later author. Waser does not represent the false shekel with the censer, but it is worth while to glance at his method of dealing with Hebrew coins. On p. 77 and elsewhere he illustrates what (reading hastily) one would take to be a halfshekel of the second year, a one-third-shekel of the third year (Fig. 5), and a quarter-shekel of the fourth year. The peculiarity about these illustrations is that while the types and legends are as well represented as in the case of the whole shekel, the letter *sh* (initial of *shenath*, year) is omitted before the numeral. Now, the only genuine shekels and halfshekels on which this initial is absent are those of the first year. Waser lets the cat out of the bag when he comes to the onethird-shekel (p. 78). Of the existence of

this as a coin we have no evidence; but
Waser says: "It is probable that the types
and symbols of this coin were the same as
those of the whole shekel, so I figure it here
with the same types, but with this different
inscription on the reverse: *shelishith hasshekel
Israel,* 'third of the shekel of Israel.'" He
does not commit himself to any statement
that the coin exists; but "it pleases him" to
represent it—"quare libet etiam eisdem
(notis et symbolis) eum figuratum hic ex-
hibere." In the same spirit he has invented
and figured the half-shekel and quarter-
shekel; for, although half-shekels exist, there
is no doubt, from his mistake in the representation of the date, that he had never seen
a half-shekel.[1] Indeed, he admits (p. 71) that
all the many shekels he had ever seen had
the letter *aleph* over the cup, *i.e.* were of the
first year; and it is a curious fact that by far

---

[1] The nature of Waser's method was recognized by J.
Morin (*Exercitationes*, p. 207). "Waser's parts of the
shekel seem not to be genuine, but invented to represent
the fractions of which mention is made in the sacred
Scriptures."

the greater number of the illustrations in works of this time represent the shekel of this year. It seems that Waser, like Arias Montanus before him, regarded the *aleph* as the indication of the unit (one shekel), and therefore systematically marked his half-shekel with a *beth*, his third with a *gimel*, and his quarter with a *daleth*.[1]

To return to the track of the false shekel. Villalpandus,[2] a year before Waser, published a plate representing a number of Jewish coins, including shekels of which we have no reason to doubt the authenticity, and also one of the censer-pieces (Pl. XII.). He insists that all these pieces, without exception, are *struck :* "which is so certain and clear upon examination, that should any one attempt to deny it, he would prove beyond all dispute that he was so lacking in knowledge of coins as to be unable to distinguish or separate

---

[1] J. B. Villalpandus, *Apparatus Urbis ac Templi Hierosolymitani*, Tom. iii., parts 1 and 2 (Rome, 1604), p. 390, recognized the inadequacy of Montanus's explanations, but proposed a worse one himself.

[2] *Op. cit.*, plate facing p. 378 ; see also p. 390.

struck coins from such as are cast or made by any other means." In the face of this fearful threat, I hesitate to assert that Villalpandus was mistaken in regard to the censerpiece; but his experience, so far as I can discover, is unique. He admits that some doubt has been thrown on the piece; but while he allows that it is somewhat later than the others which he illustrates, bearing letters of an older form, he still maintains that it is ancient.

Farther back than this I have failed to trace illustrations of this mysterious piece; but there is little doubt that something of the kind must have existed in the middle of the sixteenth century. Writing on March 21, 1552, to George III., Prince of Anhalt, Melanchthon says [1] :—

"I now send you a silver shekel of the true weight of the shekel, to wit, a tetradrachm, with the inscription as it is depicted in the book of Postellus. I also add some verses, interpreting the rod of Aaron and the pot of incense . . .

---

[1] Bretschneider, *Corpus Reformatorum*, vol. vii. p. 964; cp. vol. x. p. 607.

## DE VETERI NOMISMATE GENTIS
## IUDAICAE.

Iusta sacerdotum demonstrat munera *Siclus*
Cuius in *Ebraeis* urbibus usus erat.
Ut sint doctrinae custodes, virga *Aharonis*,
Utque regant mores cum pietate, monet.
Significantque preces calicis fragrantia thura,
Praecipuum munus sunt pia vota Deo, etc."

The verses are quoted by Waser to show
that Melanchthon considered the chalice on
the shekel (the true shekel, as he thinks) to
be not the pot of manna, but a censer.

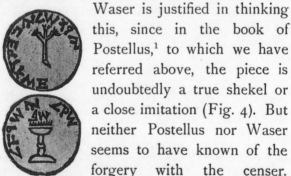

Waser is justified in thinking
this, since in the book of
Postellus,[1] to which we have
referred above, the piece is
undoubtedly a true shekel or
a close imitation (Fig. 4). But
neither Postellus nor Waser
seems to have known of the
forgery with the censer.

FIG. 4.

Melanchthon, admirable
scholar as he was, lived before the days of
scientific numismatics ; and if he had one of

---

[1] *Linguarum duodecim Alphabetum* (Paris, 1538).

the censer-pieces before him, we shall not be unjust in supposing that he would identify it with the shekel as represented by Postellus. Otherwise it is difficult to understand how he would imagine that a censer was represented.

We may conclude, therefore, that the censer-shekel existed in 1552 A.D. That it was made much earlier the style of the work forbids us to believe.

FIG 5.

# INDEX

THE END

# HEBREW ALPHABET & EQUIVALENTS.

| Name. | Form. | Sound. | General Coin Form [1]. | Number. |
|---|---|---|---|---|
| Aleph | א | Smooth breathing | | 1 |
| Beth | ב | B | | 2 |
| Gimel | ג | G | | 3 |
| Daleth | ד | D | | 4 |
| He | ה | H | | 5 |
| Vau | ו | V | | 6 |
| Zayin | ז | Z | | 7 |
| Heth | ח | H | | 8 |
| Teth | ט | Ṭ | none | 9 |
| Yodh | י | Ẏ | | 10 |
| Kaph | ך כ | K | | 20 |
| Lamedh | ל | L | | 30 |
| Mem | ם מ | M | | 40 |
| Nun | ן נ | N | | 50 |
| Samekh | ס | Ṣ | none | 60 |
| Ayin | ע | Aspirate | ◇ | 70 |
| Pe | פ | P | none | 80 |
| Çadha | צ | SS | | 90 |
| Qoph | ק | Q | | 100 |
| Resh | ר | R | | 200 |
| Shin | ש | SH | | 300 |
| Tau | ת | T | X | 400 |

1. The coin forms are only general : most letters present variations.
2. The Hebrews used no vowel signs .

# GREEK ALPHABET & EQUIVALENTS.

| Name. | Form. | Sound. | General Coin Form. | Number. |
|---|---|---|---|---|
| Alpha | A | A | A Λ | 1 |
| Beta | B | B | ΄B | 2 |
| Gamma | Γ | G | Γ | 3 |
| Delta | Δ | D | Δ | 4 |
| Epsilon | E | E | E Є | 5 |
| Zeta | Z | Z | Ι | 7 |
| Eta | H | EE | H | 8 |
| Theta | Θ | TH | Θ | 9 |
| Iota | I | I | I | 10 |
| Kappa | K | K | K | 20 |
| Lamda | Λ | L | Λ | 30 |
| Mu | M | M | M | 40 |
| Nu | N | N | N | 50 |
| Xi | Ξ | X | Ξ | 60 |
| Omicron | O | O (short) | O | 70 |
| Pi | Π | P | Π | 80 |
| Rho | P | R | P | 100 |
| Sigma | Σ | S | Σ C Ⅽ | 200 |
| Tau | T | T | T | 300 |
| Upsilon | Υ | U | Y | 400 |
| Phi | Φ | PH | Φ | 500 |
| Chi | X | CH | X | 600 |
| Psi | Ψ | PS | Ψ | 700 |
| Omega | Ω | O long | Ω ω | 800 |

1. The aspirate at the beginning of a word is represented by an inverted comma thus ὁ = ho.

2. The sign for 6 is ς (*stigma*), an obsolete *vau*: for 90 is Ϙ, an obsolete *koppa* so the sign for 900 is Ϡ (*san*).

A thousand is written ͵α.

Numerals are often preceded by the sign L : or the word ΕΤΟΥΣ.

# THE HEBREW LEGENDS.

## EARLY SHEKELS AND HALF SHEKELS.

Obv.

1. ‫ירושלם קדשה‬
*Jerushalem Kedoshah*
Holy Jerusalem.

} First year shekels
and
half shekels.

2. ‫ירושלום הקדושה‬
*Jerushalaim ha-Kedoshah*
Jerusalem the Holy.

} The remaining
years.

Rev.

3. ‫שקל ישראל‬
*Shekel Israel*
Shekel of Israel.

} Shekels.

4. ‫חצי השקל‬
*Chatzi ha-Shekel*
Half-shekel.

} Half shekels.

Numerals.

Ⲅ = א : א - 1 : ꗉ - ב - 2 . ꔈ - ג - 3 . 4 - ד - 4 . Ⅎ - ה - 5

W = ש preceding a numeral stands for

5. ‫שנת‬ = Shenath = year.

## EARLY COPPER.

Obv.

6. ‫לגאלת ציון‬
*Lige'ullath Zion*
Of the redemption of Zion.

} on all modules.

Rev.

7. ‏רֲֵֶ⊟ ⅁⅁ᒎᖴ X५ⱳ

שנת ארבע חצי

Shenath arba Chatzi
In the fourth year, one half.

8. ⅁Ƶ⅁⅁ ⅁⅁⅁Ⅹ X५ⱳ

שנת ארבע רביע

Shenath arba Rebia
In the fourth year, one quarter.

9. ⅁⅁⅁Ⅹ X५ⱳ

שנת ארבע

Shenath arba
In the fourth year.

## HASHMONEAN FAMILY.

John Hyrcanus.
Rev.
10.

| A | A |
| --- | --- |
| ⅃⅃Β₮₮Z | יהו וחנן |
| ₮₮⅃⅃₮⅃⅃ | הכהו הג |
| ₮₮⅃Β₮⅃ℇ | דל וחבר ה |
| ⅃₮₮₮₮Z | יהודים |

*Jehochanan Hakkohen Haggadol Vecheber Hajehudim.*
John the High Priest and the Senate of the Jews.
Rev.
11.

| | יהוכ |
| --- | --- |
| | נג הכהן |
| | הגדל וה |
| | בר חיה |
| | ודים |

*Jehokanan Hakkohen Haggadol Vecheber Hajehudim*
John the High Priest and the Senate of the Jews.
Rev.
12.

| | יהוכ |
| --- | --- |
| | ננהכהן ה |
| | גדל ראש |
| | הברהיה |
| | ודים |

*Jehokanan Hakkohen Haggadol Rosh Cheber Hajehudim.*
John the High Priest, Chief of the Senate of the Jews.
## JUDAS ARISTOBULUS.
Rev.
13.

| | יהוד |
| --- | --- |
| | הכהןחגד |
| | ול והבר |
| | היהודים |

*Jehudah Hakkohen Haggadol Vecheber Hajeduhim.*
Judas the High Priest and Senate of the Jews.

## ALEXANDER JANNAEUS.

Obv.

14.      𐤙𐤋𐤌𐤄 𐤉𐤗𐤊𐤘𐤄𐤆

יהונתן המלך

*Jehonathan Hammelek.*
Jonathan The King.

Rev.

15.
| 𐤙+𐤄𐤆 | ינתז |
| 𐤄𐤉𐤄𐤗𐤄 | הכהן ה |
| 𐤂𐤉𐤁+𐤋𐤄𐤄 | גדל וחבר |
| 𐤙𐤆𐤄𐤄𐤋𐤄 | היהדים |

*Jonathan Hakkohen Haggadol Vecheber Hajehudim.*
Jonathan the High Priest and Senate of the Jews.

Rev.

16.
| 𐤅 𐤄 𐤆 | יהו |
| ..... 𐤉𐤗𐤘 | נתן.. |
|  | ..... |
|  | .... .. |

*Jehonathan &c.*
Jehonathan (or Jonathan) &c.

Obv.

17.      𐤙𐤋𐤌𐤄 𐤉𐤗𐤄𐤙𐤄𐤆

והונתן המיך

*Jehonathan Hammelek.*
Jonathan the King

## ALEXANDRA.

Rev.

18.      𐤄𐤗 = ת    and other letters, perhaps

𐤅𐤗𐤙𐤋𐤅    = מלכתא = Queen

## ALEXANDER II.

Rev.

19.   ⁣ *Lᴧ7ᴅᴧ99ᴣᴌᴅ*   גדל (עש)עלצדר

*Alexandras Gadol.*
Alexander great (high Priest).

## ANTIGONUS.

Obv.

20.   ⁣ *ᴤᴝᴧᴄᴧᴣᴣᴣ 99ᴃᴜᴄ99ᴣ ᴣᴣᴣᴣ ᴣᴣᴧᴄᴄᴤ*
מתתיה הכהך הגדל והבר היהודים

*Mattathiah Hakkohen Haggadol Vecheber Hajehudim.*
Matthias the High Priest and Senate of the Jews.

   ⁣ *ᴛᴜ*   ‎שא. = First year.
   ⁣ *ᴣᴜ*   ‎שב. = Second year.

## FIRST REVOLT.

Obv.

21.   ⁣ *ᴤᴣᴝᴄ ᴝᴣᴤᴣ*   שנת שתים

*Shenath shtayim.* Year two.

22.   ⁣ *ᴝᴜᴄᴝ ᴝᴣᴤᴝ*   שנת שלוש

*Shenath shalosh.* Year three.

Rev.

23.   ⁣ *ᴣᴝᴣᴣ ᴝᴣᴃ*   חרות ציון

*Cheruth Zion*
Deliverance of Zion

## SECOND REVOLT.

Obv.

24.   ⁣ *ᴣᴣᴣᴣᴣ99ᴣᴄᴛ*   אלעזר הכהז

(usually retrograde).
*Eleazar Hakkohen.*
Eleazar the Priest.

25.

ᴎ×◁ꟼW     שמעון
ꟻⱿWᏏ     נשיא
ᒪꟻꟼWᏠ     ישראל

*Shimoun Nasi Israel.*
Simon Prince of Israel.

26.
     ᴎꟼOᏏW
or
     ꟼ×OᏏW      שביעו (for שמעון.)

*Shimoun.*
Simon.

27.      Ꮟᒪ(ᴎ×ꟻᏠ     ירושלם

*Jerushalem.*
Jerusalem.
Rev.

28.      ᒪꟻꟼWᏃ ×ᒪꟻᏃᒪ ×Ɐꟻ× ×Ꮪᴎ
שנת אחת לגאלת ישראל

*Shenath achath Lige‘ullath Israel*
First year of the redemption of Israel

29.      ᒪꟻꟼWᏃ [×ᴎ]ꟼⱯᒪꟻW
שב לחר [ות] ישראל

*Schin Beth. Lecheruth Israel.*
Second year of the deliverance of Israel.

30.      Ꮟᒪ(ᴎ×ꟻᏃ ××ꟼⱯᒪᴢ     לחרות ירושלם

*Lecheruth Jerushalem.*
Of the deliverance of Jerusalem.

# GREEK LEGENDS.

## HASHMONEAN FAMILY

*Time of John Hyrcanus.*

31. ΒΑΣΙΛΕΩΣ ΑΝΤΙΟΧΟΥ ΕΥΕΡΓΕΤΟΥ.
[Money of] King Antiochus the Benefactor (Antiochus VII of Syria). Two dates.
ΑΠΡ. = Era of Seleucidae 181 = B.C. 132.
ΒΠΡ. =            —            182 = B.C. 131.

*Alexander Jannaeus.*

32. Rev. ΒΑΣΙΛΕΩΣ ΑΛΕΞΑΝΔΡΟΥ.
[Money of] King Alexander.

*Alexandra.*

33. ΒΑΣΙΛΙΣ ΑΛΕΞΑΝΔ.
[Money of] Queen Alexandra.

*Antigonus.*

34. Rev. ΒΑΣΙΛΕΩΣ ΑΝΤΙΓΟΝΟΥ.
[Money of] King Antigonus.

## HEROD FAMILY

*Herod the Great.*

35. ΒΑΣΙΛΕΩΣ ·ΗΡΩΔΟΥ.
[Money of] King Herod.
Date ΛΓ = year three.
₱ τρίχαλκον = Three chalcoi.

*Herod Archelaus.*

36. ΗΡΩ ΔΟΥ ΕΘΝΑΡΧΟΥ.
[Money of] Herod the Ethnarch.

*Herod Antipas.*

37. Obv. ΗΡΩΔΟΥ ΤΕΤΡΑΡΧΟΥ.
[Money of] Herod the Tetrarch.
Dates Λ ΜΓ or Λ ΜΔ year 43 or 44 or ΕΤΟ[ΥΣ] ΜΓ of the
year 43.

38. Rev. ΤΙΒΕΡΙΑC.
Tiberias (on Lake Gennesareth).

39. Rev. ΓΑΙΩ ΚΑΙϹΑΡΙ ΓΕΡΜΑΝΙΚΩ ΣΕΒ[ΑΣΤΙ].
In the reign of Caius Caesar Germanicus Augustus.

40. Obv. ΚΑΙϹΑΡΙ ϹΕΒΑϹΤ U (*sic*).
In the reign of Augustus Caesar.

41. Obv. ΤΙΒΕΡΙΟϹ ϹΕΒΑϹΤΟϹ ΚΑΙϹΑΡ.
[Money of] Tiberius Augustus Caesar.

42. Rev. ΦΙΛΙΠΠΟΥ ΤΕΤΡΑΡΧΟΥ.
[Money of] Philip the Tetrarch.
Reverse bears date.

L IB = year 12.
L IϹ = — ·16.
L IΘ = — 19.
L ΛΓ = — 33.
L ΛΖ = — 37.

*Herod Agrippa I.*

43. Obv. ΒΑϹΙΛΕΩϹ ΑΓΡΙΠΑ.
[Money of] King Agrippa.
Rev. L Ϲ = year 6.

**PROCURATORS**.

44. Obv. ΚΑΙϹΑΡΟϹ.
Money of Caesar.
Rev. L ΛΓ = year 33.    Coponius
     L ΛϹ = — 36.
     L ΛΘ = — 39. ⎱ Marcus Ambivius
     L Μ = — 40. ⎰ Annius Rufus.
     L ΜΑ = — 41.

*Valerius Gratus.*

45. Obv. ΙΟΥΛ-ϹΕΒ.
[Money of] Julia Augusta.

46. ΚΑΙϹΑΡ.
[Money of] Caesar.

47. ΤΙΒΕΡΙΟΥ.
[Money of] Tiberius.

48. ΤΙΒ·ΚΑΙϹΑΡ.
[Money of] Tiberius Caesar.

49. **TIBEPIOY KAICAPOC**. With date **L·IS** = year 16.
[Money of] Tiberius Caesar.

50. Rev. **TIB**.
[Money of] Tiberius.

51. **KAICAP**.
[Money of] Caesar.

52. **IOYΛIA**.
[Money of] Julia.

53. **IOYΛIA KAICAPOC**.
[Money of] Julia Augusta.
Dates. **L Γ** year 3.
    **L Δ** year 4.
    **L E** — 5.
    **L IA** — 11.
    **L IS** — 16.
    **L IZ** — 17. } Pontius Pilate.
    **L IH** — 18.

*Claudius Felix.*

54. Obv. **TI KΛAYΔIOC KAICAP ΓEPM**.
[Money of] Titus Claudius Caesar Germanicus.

55. **NEPω KΛAY KAICAP**.
[Money of] Nero Claudius Caesar.

56. Rev. **IOYΛIA AΓPIΠΠINA**.
[Money of] Julia Agrippina.

57. **BPIT·KAI**.
[Money of] Britannicus Caesar.
Date. **L IΔ**. Year 14.

58. *Porcius Festus.*
Obv. **L E KAICAPOC**.
Year 5 [Money of] Caesar.

59. Rev. **NEPωNOΣ**.
[Money of] Nero.

**AFTER FIRST REVOLT.**

Roman money commemorating Victory.

*Vespasian.*

60. Obv. ΑΥΤΟΚΡ ΟΥΕΣΠ ΚΑΙ ΣΕΒ.
[Money of] the Emperor Vespasian Caesar Augustus.

61. Rev. ΙΟΥΔΑΙΑ⳽ ΕΑΛⲰΚΥΙΑΣ.
On the conquest of Judaea.

*Titus.*

62. Rev. ΑΥΤΟΚΡ ΤΙΤΟ⳽ ΚΑΙΣΑΡ ΣΕΒ.
[Money of] the Emperor Titus Caesar Augustus.

63. Rev. ΙΟΥΔΑΙΑΣ· ΕΑΛⲰΚΥΙΑΣ.
On the Conquest of Judaea.


## LATIN LEGENDS.

*Vespasian.*

64. Obv. IMP.CAES.VESPASIANVS.AVG :
Imperator Caesar Vespasianus Augustus.
The Emperor Caesar Vespasian Augustus.

65. TP.P.
Tribunitia Potestate. With the Tribunitian power.

66. P.M. or PONT.MAX.
Pontifex Maximus. Chief Priest.

67. COS.
Consul(followed by numeral indicating the year of the Consulate)

68. P.P.
Pater Patriae. His Country's Father.

69. CENS or CENSOR.
Censor.

70. DIVVS AVGVSTVS VESPASIANVS.
The Divine Augustus Vespasian (issued on his death and consequent deification).

71. Rev. VICT.AVG. or VICTORIA AVGVSTI.
Victoria Augusti.
The Victory of Augustus.

72. IVDAEA CAPTA, or sometimes IVDAEA only, or IVD
CAP.
The captivity of Judaea.

73. IVDAEA DEVICTA.
The conquest of Judaea.

74. DE IVDAEIS.
In the matter of the Jews.

75. EX.S.C.
Ex Senatus consulto.
By command of the Senate.

76. TRIVMP.AVG.
Triumphus Augusti.
The triumph of Augustus.

77. VICTORIA NAVALIS.
The naval victory.

*Titus.*

78. Obv. IMP.T.CAESAR VESPASIANVS.
TR.POT.AVG.P.M.COS.P.P.CENSOR exactly the same as
above but T stands for Titus.

79. AVG.F is Augusti Filius — the son of Augustus.
Rev. Similar legends to Vespasian except:

80. IVDAEA NAVALIS.
Judaea sea conquered.

*Domitian.*

81. Obv. IMP.CAES.DOMIT.AVG.GERM.
Imperator Caesar Domitianus Augustus Germanicus, with offices
as Vespasian and Titus.

82. Rev. VICTOR AVG.
Victoria Augusti.
The Victory of Augustus.

*Nerva.*

83. Obv. IMP.NERVA CAES.AVG.P.M.TR.P.COS.III P.P.

The emperor Nerva, Caesar, Augustus, Chief Priest endowed with the Tribunitian Power, Consul for the third time, Father of his country.

84. Rev. FISCI IVDAICI CALVMNIA SVBLATA.
[To commemorate] the removal of the scandal of the Jewish Tax.

*Hadrian.*

85. Obv. HADRIANVS.AVG.COS.III.P.P.
Hadrianus Augustus Consul III Pater patriae.
Hadrian Augustus Consul for the third time, his country's Father.

86. Rev. ADVENTVI AVG.IVDAEAE.
[To commemorate] the arrival of Augustus in Judaea.

87. S.C.IVDAEA.
By command of the Senate. Judaea.

———————

PLATES

PLATE I.

PLATE II.

*To face page* 24.

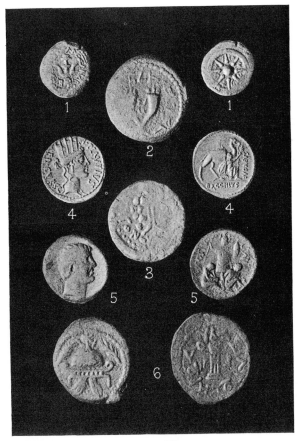

PLATE III.

*To face page* 30.

PLATE IV.

*To face page* 34.

PLATE V.

*To face page* 42.

PLATE VI.

To face page 46.

PLATE VII.

*To face page* 48.

PLATE VIII.

*To face page* 54.

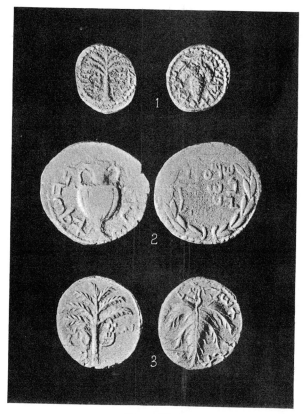

PLATE IX.

*To face page* 56.

PLATE X.

*To face page* 60.

PLATE XI.

*To face page* 61.

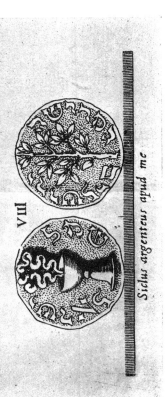

ISRAEL SICLVS: SANCTA IERVSALEM

viii

Siclus argenteus apud me

PLATE XII.

To face page 70.